THE ROCK

BY MATT SCHEFF

PRO WRESTLING
SUPERSTARS

Published by ABDO Publishing Company, PO Box 398166, Minneapolis, MN 55439. Copyright © 2014 by Abdo Consulting Group, Inc. International copyrights reserved in all countries. No part of this book may be reproduced in any form without written permission from the publisher. SportsZone™ is a trademark and logo of ABDO Publishing Company.

Printed in the United States of America,
North Mankato, Minnesota
082013
012014

Editor: Chrös McDougall
Series Designer: Jake Nordby

Photo Credits: WWE/AP Images, cover, 1, 28-29, 30 (bottom); Paul Abell/ AP Images for WWE Corp., cover (background), 1 (background), 18 (inset); Zuma Press/Icon SMI, 4-5, 15 (inset); Marc Serota/AP Images, 6-7, 10-11, 14-15, 26-27, 31; Mike Lano Photojournalism, 7 (inset), 12, 13, 20-21, 23 (inset), 30 (top); Jeffrey Boan/AP Images, 8-9; George Pimentel/WireImage/ Getty Images, 16-17; WWF, Stuart Ramson/AP Images, 18-19; Richard Drew/AP Images, 22-23; Walt Disney Pictures/Album/Newscom, 24-25

Library of Congress Control Number: 2013945678

Cataloging-in-Publication Data

Scheff, Matt.
  The Rock / Matt Scheff.
    p. cm. -- (Pro wrestling superstars)
  Includes index.
  ISBN 978-1-62403-139-7
  1. Johnson, Dwayne, 1972- --Juvenile literature. 2. Wrestlers--United States-- Biography--Juvenile literature. 3. Actors-- United States--Biography--Juvenile literature. 1. Title.
  796.812092--dc23
  [B]

                                                                2013945678

CONTENTS

The Rock is a WWE legend.

EIGHT-TIME CHAMP

The Rock was in trouble. He was battling CM Punk for the World Wrestling Entertainment (WWE) championship. A group called the Shield rushed out to help Punk. They slammed the Rock into a table.

WWE chairman Vince McMahon came to the ring as Punk celebrated. McMahon told the crowd that he was giving the belt to the Rock. But the Rock refused it. He wanted to *earn* the title. And that's what he did. He hit Punk in the face with the People's Elbow and covered Punk for the pin. It was the Rock's eighth WWE championship!

Fast Fact

The Rock's victory ended CM Punk's amazing title reign of 434 days!

Johnson dreamed of playing football growing up.

FAST FACT

Johnson's family moved a lot because of his dad's wrestling career. Dwayne lived in five different states before he started kindergarten.

YOUNG DWAYNE JOHNSON

The Rock's real name is Dwayne Johnson. He was born on May 2, 1972, in Hayward, California. Johnson came from a wrestling family. His father and grandfather had both wrestled.

Johnson was a good athlete. But he wasn't interested in wrestling. His real love was football. He was a star defensive tackle in high school.

Johnson's father was a wrestler named Rocky Johnson.

Johnson accepted a football scholarship to the University of Miami in Florida. He was a good player. He helped Miami win the national championship in 1992. But Johnson hurt his back during his final season. His college football career was over. Johnson still hoped to get a chance in the National Football League (NFL). However, no NFL team picked him in the draft.

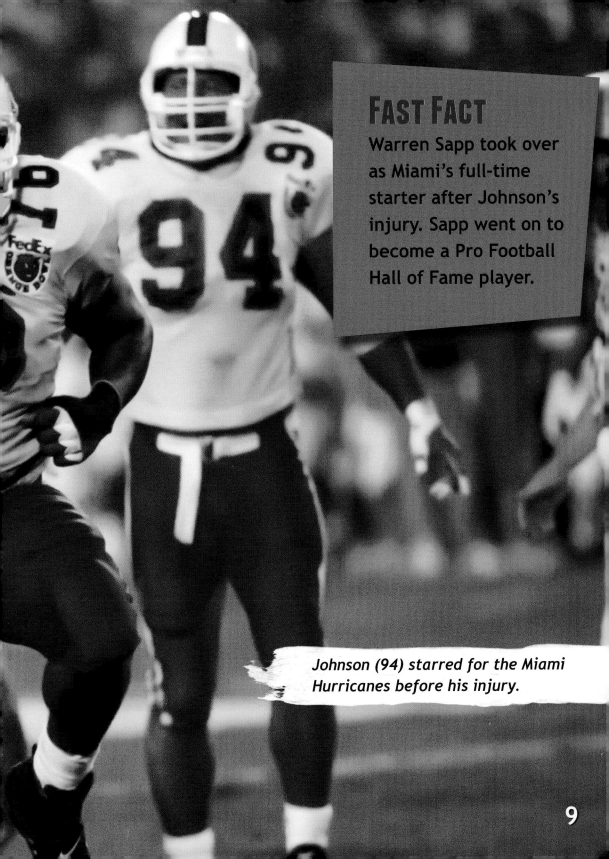

FAST FACT

Warren Sapp took over as Miami's full-time starter after Johnson's injury. Sapp went on to become a Pro Football Hall of Fame player.

Johnson (94) starred for the Miami Hurricanes before his injury.

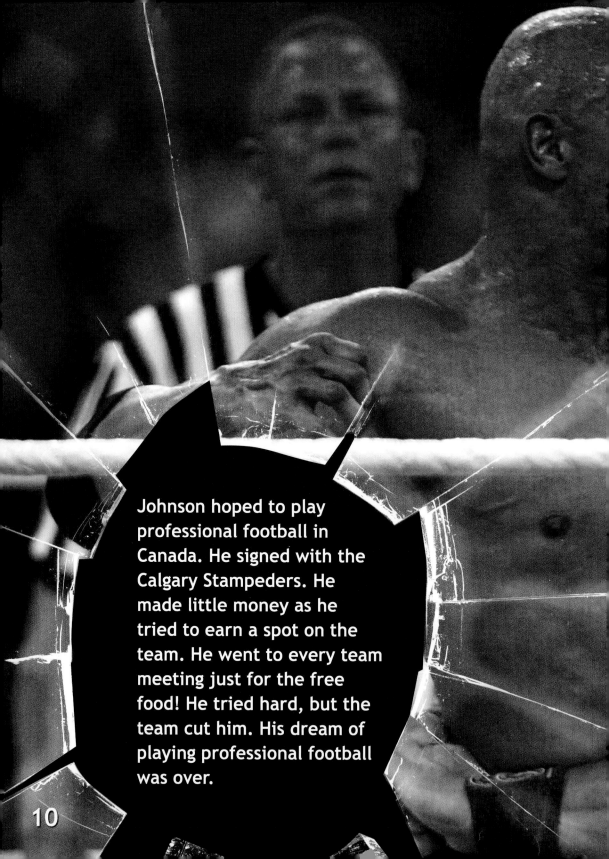

Johnson hoped to play professional football in Canada. He signed with the Calgary Stampeders. He made little money as he tried to earn a spot on the team. He went to every team meeting just for the free food! He tried hard, but the team cut him. His dream of playing professional football was over.

The Rock punches John Cena at WrestleMania 28.

Johnson looked to pro wrestling for a career after football.

Johnson had no job and no money. He moved back into his parents' home. He talked his father into training him to become a wrestler.

Johnson wrestled as Flex Kavana in a small league called the United States Wrestling Alliance. In 1996, WWE signed Johnson to a contract. He would wrestle as Rocky Maivia.

The Rock makes a grand entrance.

FAST FACT

Johnson's father wrestled as Rocky Johnson. Johnson's grandfather was Peter Maivia. The name *Rocky Maivia* was a combination of the two.

THE ROCK IS BORN

Maivia was an instant hit. His first match was in November 1996. It was an eight-way battle with many experienced wrestlers. Maivia won! Just three months later, he beat Hunter Hearst Helmsley to win the intercontinental championship.

The Rock flies at John Cena during WrestleMania 28.

The Rock rose to WWE stardom.

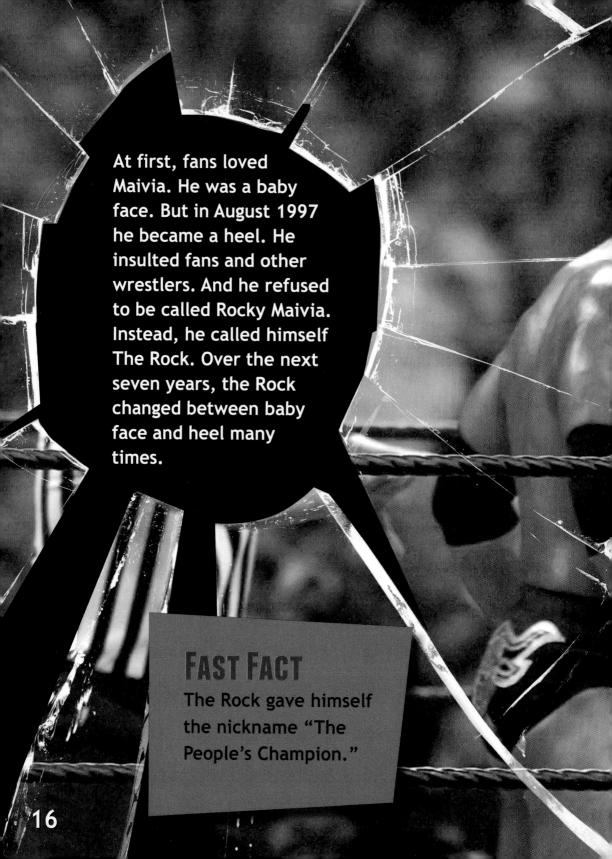

At first, fans loved Maivia. He was a baby face. But in August 1997 he became a heel. He insulted fans and other wrestlers. And he refused to be called Rocky Maivia. Instead, he called himself The Rock. Over the next seven years, the Rock changed between baby face and heel many times.

FAST FACT
The Rock gave himself the nickname "The People's Champion."

The Rock faces up against Hulk Hogan at WrestleMania 18.

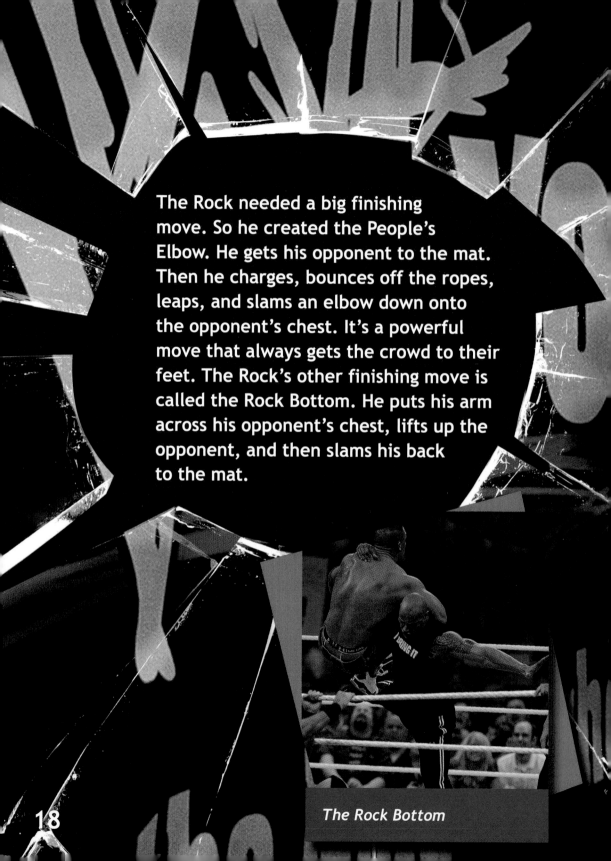

The Rock needed a big finishing move. So he created the People's Elbow. He gets his opponent to the mat. Then he charges, bounces off the ropes, leaps, and slams an elbow down onto the opponent's chest. It's a powerful move that always gets the crowd to their feet. The Rock's other finishing move is called the Rock Bottom. He puts his arm across his opponent's chest, lifts up the opponent, and then slams his back to the mat.

The Rock Bottom

The Rock poses outside a WWE restaurant in 2000.

FAST FACT

Before a big move, the Rock sometimes shouts to the crowd, "Do you smell what the Rock is cooking?"

THE PEOPLE'S CHAMPION

The Rock became a huge star around 1998. That's when he teamed up with WWE owner Vince McMahon. They led a stable called the Corporation. Fans hated the Rock and the Corporation. The Rock talked down to the fans and sometimes cheated. Plus he battled popular rivals in Mankind and "Stone Cold" Steve Austin. The Rock was successful, though. He often held the WWE championship belt that Mankind and Stone Cold wanted.

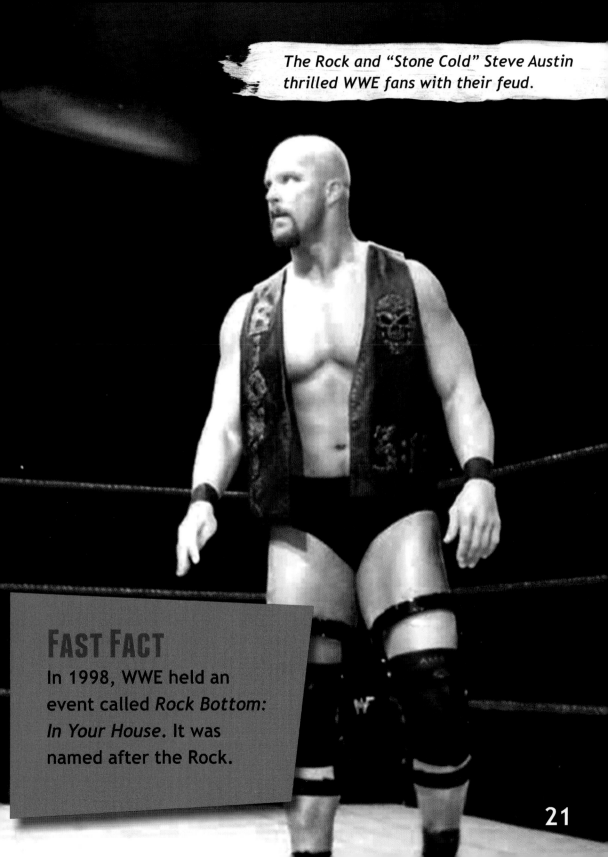

The Rock and "Stone Cold" Steve Austin thrilled WWE fans with their feud.

FAST FACT

In 1998, WWE held an event called *Rock Bottom: In Your House*. It was named after the Rock.

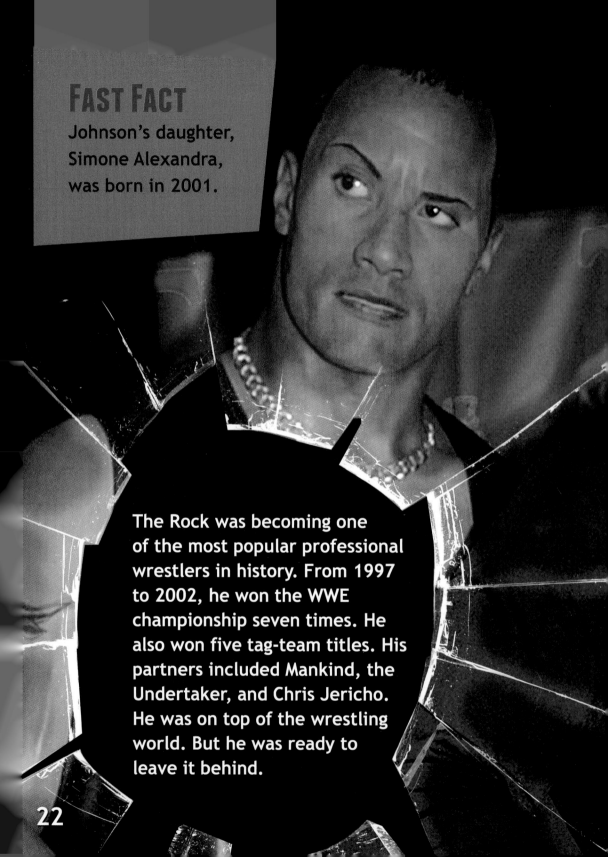

The Rock was becoming one
of the most popular professional
wrestlers in history. From 1997
to 2002, he won the WWE
championship seven times. He
also won five tag-team titles. His
partners included Mankind, the
Undertaker, and Chris Jericho.
He was on top of the wrestling
world. But he was ready to
leave it behind.

The Rock poses next to his wax likeness in 2002 at Madame Tussaud's wax museum in New York.

The People's Champ

Johnson acts in Race to Witch Mountain.

Fast Fact

The Rock's films include *The Rundown* (2003), *Get Smart* (2008), *Race to Witch Mountain* (2009), and *Fast & Furious 6* (2013).

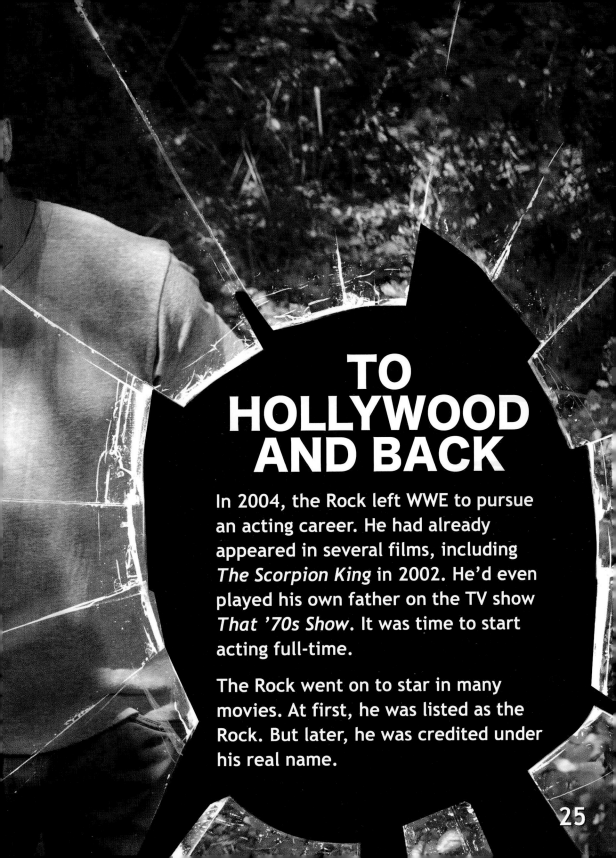

TO HOLLYWOOD AND BACK

In 2004, the Rock left WWE to pursue an acting career. He had already appeared in several films, including *The Scorpion King* in 2002. He'd even played his own father on the TV show *That '70s Show*. It was time to start acting full-time.

The Rock went on to star in many movies. At first, he was listed as the Rock. But later, he was credited under his real name.

FAST FACT

The Rock appeared on the TV show *Star Trek: Voyager* in 2000. He played an alien wrestler who used the Rock's moves!

The Rock didn't leave WWE behind entirely. He appeared as a guest sometimes. In 2011, he made fun of WWE star John Cena. The two started a feud. The Rock decided to return to the ring. He and Cena finally faced off in 2012 at WrestleMania. Cena tried to use the People's Elbow on the Rock. But it didn't work. The Rock slammed Cena to the mat with a Rock Bottom to win the match.

The Rock and John Cena stare each other down at WrestleMania 28.

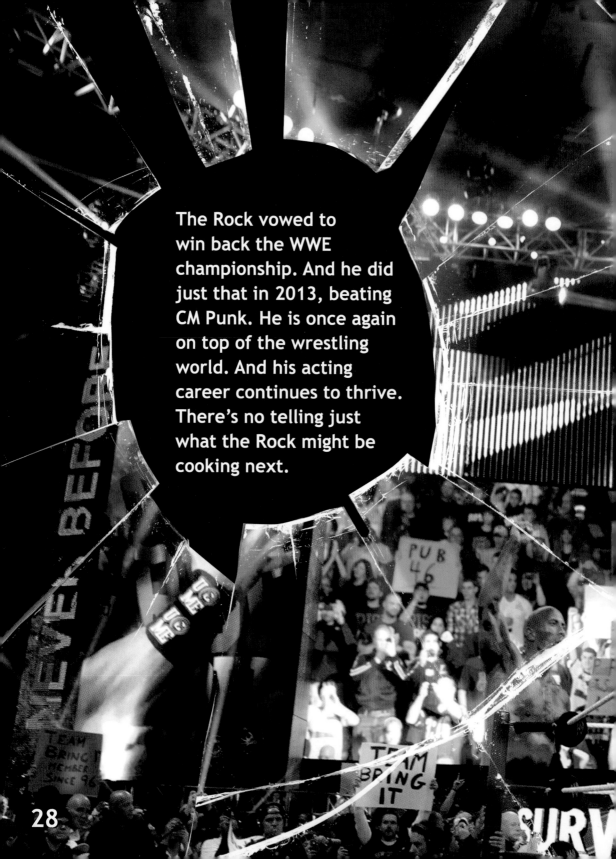

The Rock vowed to win back the WWE championship. And he did just that in 2013, beating CM Punk. He is once again on top of the wrestling world. And his acting career continues to thrive. There's no telling just what the Rock might be cooking next.

The Rock will go down in history as "The People's Champion."

FAST FACT

In 2013, the Rock helped create and hosted the TV game show *The Hero*.

TIMELINE

1972
Dwayne Johnson is born May 2 in Hayward, California.

1992
Johnson wins college football's national championship with the University of Miami.

1996
Johnson signs with WWE and wins his first match.

1997
The Rock, wrestling as Rocky Maivia, wins his first WWE belt, the intercontinental championship.

2002
The Rock's first big movie, *The Scorpion King*, is released.

2004
The Rock leaves WWE to pursue an acting career.

2012
The Rock returns to WWE and defeats John Cena at WrestleMania.

2013
The Rock defeats CM Punk to earn his eighth WWE championship.

GLOSSARY

baby face
A wrestler whom fans view as a good guy.

contract
An agreement between two parties who are working together.

defensive tackle
In football, a defender who begins each play on the line of scrimmage, across from the offensive guards or center.

feud
An intense, long-lasting conflict between two wrestlers.

finishing move
A powerful move that a wrestler uses to finish off an opponent.

heel
A wrestler whom fans view as a villain.

rival
An opponent with whom a wrestler has an intense competition.

scholarship
Financial assistance awarded to students to help them pay for school. Top athletes earn scholarships to represent a college through its sports teams.

stable
A group of wrestlers who work together.

INDEX